What in the World Do You Do When Your Parents Divorce?

A Survival Guide for Kids

What in the World Do You Do When Your Parents Divorce?

A Survival Guide for Kids

Kent Winchester and Roberta Beyer

Edited by Elizabeth Verdick

free spirit
PUBLiSHiNG®

Works
for kids®

Library of Congress Cataloging-in-Publication Data

Winchester, Kent.
    What in the world do you do when your parents divorce? : a survival guide for kids / Kent Winchester and Roberta Beyer.
        p. cm.
    Also issued as a component of a kit entitled Juggling act.
    ISBN 1-57542-092-9 (pbk.)
    1. Children of divorced parents—Psychology—Juvenile literature. 2. Divorce—Juvenile liter-ature. [1. Divorce.] I. Beyer, Roberta, 1951– II. Title.

HQ777.5 .W55 2001
306.89—dc21   2001023029

At the time of this book's publication, all facts and figures cited are the most current available; all telephone numbers, addresses, and Web site URLs are accurate and active; all publications, organ-izations, Web sites, and other resources exist as described in this book; and all have been verified. The authors and Free Spirit Publishing make no warranty or guarantee concerning the informa-tion and materials given out by organizations or content found at Web sites, and we are not responsible for any changes that occur after this book's publication. If you find an error or believe that a resource listed here is not as described, please contact Free Spirit Publishing. Parents, teach-ers, and other adults: we strongly urge you to monitor children's use of the Internet.

Illustrations by Marieka Heinlen

10 9 8 7 6 5 4 3 2
Printed in Canada

Free Spirit Publishing Inc.
217 Fifth Avenue North, Suite 200
Minneapolis, MN 55401-1299
(612) 338-2068
help4kids@freespirit.com
www.freespirit.com

This book is dedicated to Ian and Shauna,
who know what it is to have divorced parents.
I wish you had this book when your mom and I
got divorced. It might have made it easier for you.
I love you.
Kent Winchester

To my good friend and talented collaborator
on the My Two Homes project, Cyd Riley.
Roberta Beyer

Acknowledgments

This book was helped along the way by many people. Gale made us laugh when we needed to laugh. Shelly deserves several sets of angel wings for her patience and hard work on the manuscripts. Dr. Lou Kodituwaaku generously shared with us her considerable knowledge and wisdom about children of divorce and their needs, and was always available to answer our questions. Jan Zimmerman believed in the My Two Homes products and offered constant encouragement along the way. We thank them all. Finally, we want to thank all of the children who shared their words and wisdom with us.

Contents

Introduction

What in the World Do You Do When Your Parents Divorce? is for kids whose parents have decided not to live together anymore. If your parents are breaking up, separating, getting divorced, or recently divorced, you probably have lots of questions about what's happening. This book was written to give you some answers.

Divorce is hard on everyone involved. You may have felt really shocked or confused when you first heard that your parents weren't going to be married any longer. You may have felt angry, scared, and lonely all at the same time. You may have felt sad to learn that one of your parents would be living in a different home. Divorce is a big change for everyone. Big changes—even if they turn out to be good ones in the long run—can be scary. You may wonder if you'll ever be okay again. You will be. In time, things will get better.

We both have lots of experience in the area of divorce. Roberta has helped hundreds of people handle their divorces. Kent got divorced ten years ago when his two children were ages four and eight. We decided to write a book about divorce just for kids, so we could help you understand and get through your parents' divorce.

This book is based on some of the most common questions that children ask when their parents are divorcing. Each section starts with a question, followed by answers that can help you. Along with these answers, we've also provided words from kids whose parents have gone through divorce. (We didn't use any of the kids' names, for privacy reasons.) You'll discover what these other kids have to say, how they've coped, and what advice they can offer about handling divorce. If you need more information, take a look at some of the suggested resources we recommend throughout the book. Even more important, talk to someone who can help you. Find an adult who will listen and can give you advice.

If you still have questions and are looking for answers, you can write to us at:

Kent Winchester and Roberta Beyer
Free Spirit Publishing Inc.
217 Fifth Avenue North, Suite 200
Minneapolis, MN 55401-1299

Or email us care of:
help4kids@freespirit.com

We look forward to hearing from you!

Kent Winchester and Roberta Beyer

What does it mean to get a divorce?

Maybe this is the first time you've heard the word *divorce* or thought it had anything to do with you. What does it mean? Divorce is a legal word for the end of a marriage. Parents who get divorced aren't married to each other any longer. They sign legal papers saying the marriage is over and they won't be living in the same home. Moms and dads who divorce can marry other people someday, if they choose. Even though divorce is a little word, it means big changes are happening.

There's one thing that a divorce *can't* change, though. You still have a family—even though your parents will now live in two different places. A divorce ends your parents' marriage, but it's not the end of your family. Your family is still your family. Nothing can change that.

Why do some parents divorce?

You probably thought your parents would be together forever. They probably thought so, too. When your parents
first met, they liked each other a lot. They spent more and
more time together, and their feelings for each other grew
stronger. They married and had a family. When they wel-
comed you into their life, they probably never thought
they'd be divorced. The day you were born or adopted was
one of the best days they ever had.

Parents don't stop loving their children. But sometimes,
parents stop loving each other the way they once did.
Adults can change in ways that make it difficult for them to
stay happy together. Maybe one parent has problems that
aren't being solved. Maybe both parents fight a lot or can't
agree about how to live together. They might feel unhappy
or have trouble working things out. If their feelings of love
for each other change, parents may decide they can't be in
the same home anymore.

Sometimes parents can still be friends after a divorce. Other times, they don't stay friends. Even though it might not feel like it to you, your parents made their decision to divorce because they thought it would make everyone happier in the long run.

One thing is for sure: divorces are *grown-up solutions for grown-up problems*. Your mom and dad aren't divorcing *you*—they're divorcing each other. Your parents haven't stopped loving you. Always remember that.

If you don't know why your parents are getting divorced, you can ask them. You might say it in one of these ways:

"Mom, why are you and Dad breaking up?"

"Dad, why are you and Mom getting a divorce?"

Here's a resource that can help you understand some basics about divorce:

Dinosaurs Divorce: A Guide for Changing Families by Laurene Krasny Brown and Marc Brown (Boston: Little, Brown and Company, 1988). You may be familiar with Marc Brown's illustrations of the Arthur and D.W. characters from books and TV. In *Dinosaurs Divorce,* his dinosaur characters work through the many difficult feelings and changes that come with divorce. You'll learn about why divorce happens, what it's like to have two homes, and much more.

Is it okay to talk about the divorce?

The answer is YES! It's healthy to talk about it.

The truth is, it's hard for some parents to talk about divorce. They may not know what to say or how to say it. This is an emotional time for them. They may disagree about the reasons for the divorce. They may feel tense and upset. Sometimes, one parent wants the divorce more than the other one does. Even so, the divorce is hard on both your dad and your mom.

When your parents are confused or upset, they may find it difficult to talk with you. They may say things like, "I don't want to talk about this right now," or "Ask your mom (or ask your dad), not me." If you hear words like this, you might feel worse.

What can you do? Try to be patient with your parents. Keep asking questions until your parents help you understand why they decided to get a divorce. If you still need help with answers, see pages 32–38 for ideas about talking to other people.

> "I was confused about who wanted the divorce. My mom said my dad wanted it, but my dad said my mom wanted the divorce. They both said they wanted the fighting to stop."
>
> **BOY, 8**

Maybe you feel that you *don't* want to talk about it. Here's a book that can help:

I Don't Want to Talk About It by Jeanie Franz Ransom (Washington, DC: Magination Press, 2000). When a child's parents tell her they've decided to divorce, the last thing she wants to do is talk about it. Instead, she wants to roar as loud as a lion, so she can't hear their painful words, or she wants to turn into a fish and hide her tears in the sea. As you read this book, you'll see how the girl realizes that while some things will change because of the divorce, many things will stay the same.

Is the divorce my fault?

The divorce isn't your fault. The divorce *isn't* your fault! It's worth repeating because it's important—and it's the truth.

Many kids think *they* caused the divorce. They feel guilty, as if it's all their fault. You might feel this way yourself. For example, if your parents argue a lot, you might think that if you weren't around they might stop fighting. Maybe you believe that if you acted "better" or did more things "right" they wouldn't get a divorce. This is a big burden to put on yourself. You aren't to blame. No one is. Blame hurts—it doesn't help. Keep telling yourself the divorce isn't your fault.

It's not my fault...
It's not my fault...
It's not my fault...

Your parents aren't getting divorced because of anything you did. If you're worried about whether the divorce is your fault, talk to your mom or dad. Or talk to someone else like an aunt, an uncle, a grown-up friend, or a teacher. Share your feelings with someone you trust. Bottling up your feelings *never* helps. They stay inside you, hurting you more.

"I used to believe the divorce was all my fault. But one day I thought: Only grown-ups can cause divorces."

GIRL, 11

Here's what you can say when you talk to a parent or another adult:

"Sometimes, I think the divorce is all because of me. I think it's my fault. Will you help me?"

These books can help you understand that the divorce isn't your fault:

It's Not Your Fault, KoKo Bear by Vicki Lansky (Minnetonka, MN: Book Peddlers, 1998). This helpful book for younger kids has a character named KoKo Bear. When KoKo Bear's parents get divorced, he doesn't want to live in two homes. He learns that both of his parents still love him and will always take care of him.

Let's Talk About It: Divorce by Fred Rogers (New York: G.P. Putnam's Sons, 1996). Divorce is an adult problem, and you're not responsible for your parents' break-up. This is one of the most important messages in Mr. Rogers's book. He also explains how activities—like talking, drawing, and playing with friends—can help you deal with your feelings of sadness and anger.

What happens to our family now?

During or after the time your parents get their divorce, lots of new things will happen. You'll probably hear words like *court, judge, lawyer,* or *custody.* These words may be unfamiliar or seem strange and scary. You may not understand what they're all about. Following are some explanations that can help you.

A divorce is a legal agreement, so your dad and mom will probably hire lawyers to help them. A lawyer is a person who knows about the law. Most likely, your mom will have her own lawyer and your dad will have his own. These lawyers help your parents work out the details of their divorce. Another choice is for your parents to have a *mediator.* A mediator sits down with your parents and helps them work out the details of the divorce together.

The divorce papers need to be signed by a judge. Sometimes, judges play another role in a divorce: they make decisions for parents who don't agree. For example, a judge may decide how to divide up parents' money and belongings in a fair way. A judge is found in a court of law. The court is where the legal decisions are made. Children sometimes go to court, too, if it might help the judge decide how to help their parents.

One of the most important things your parents will decide during and after the divorce involves *you*. They need to arrange how they can both spend time with you when they live apart. A judge may tell them what schedule to follow, or they may decide this between themselves with help from lawyers or a mediator. Often, this decision is called the *custody* or *visitation* schedule. (For information about *supervised visitation,* see pages 74–75.)

The schedule can be different for each family who's going through a divorce. Some kids may live with one parent during weekdays, and then spend weekends with the other parent. Some kids may spend most of the year with one parent, and then stay with the other parent during the summer and school holidays. Some kids may spend about half of their time with each parent. Some kids may go back and forth between their parents several times a month. If you have brothers or sisters, all of you will have a schedule of when you'll see your parents.

Right now, this may seem confusing. Change can be scary—even for grown-ups. You might feel angry. You might feel as if your life is out of control. You might feel as if everyone is making decisions without asking you about them. Sometimes, you might just want to cry or scream.

"You really shouldn't start worrying unless something happens. Let the grown-ups try to figure things out. They really do care about you, and they'll try to make things work. And if they don't, that doesn't mean they don't care. They're having a hard time, too. Just remember that your parents love you, that other people love you, and that everything will be okay."

GIRL, 8

It may help to remember that some things won't change at all. For example, the love your parents have for you will stay the same. You still have a dad, and you still have a mom. They may not live in the same place anymore, but they're still your parents. You still have a family.

You can make a list of other things that won't change. For example, you'll still have your grandparents or other relatives. Maybe you'll still go to the same school and have the same friends. Maybe you'll still have your favorite pet. Keep this list nearby as a reminder of the things in your life that will stay the same. Add to the list whenever you'd like.

It might also help to tell yourself that the adults who are making decisions in the divorce will try to do what's best for you. They want you to feel safe and secure, even though so much is changing in your life. Sometimes you'll feel good about the decisions and sometimes you won't.

If you feel that your parents aren't considering what's
best for you, take a look at pages 39–43 and 73–77 for
information on how to cope.

What do I do about my feelings?

Going through a divorce is a huge change in a family. It might seem like a big storm blowing through your life. Storms can make people react in different ways: they might feel scared, upset, angry, stressed out, confused, tense, frustrated, or worried.

Often, when you've got a lot going on with your emotions, your body reacts, too. You might have stomachaches or headaches that aren't related to an illness like the flu. Some days, you may wake up not wanting to go to school. Some nights, you may have nightmares or want to crawl into bed with your dad or mom. These reactions may be closely related to your feelings.

Anger is one of the most common emotions kids feel when their parents are divorcing. You might feel like yelling as loud as you can or kicking a wall. You might feel so angry inside that you just don't know what to do. Sometimes, you might let that anger out by talking back to your parents or teachers and picking fights with others. It's best not to act out your anger through fighting or mean words.

Maybe you hide or bury your anger—but you've got to let it out. Anger needs to be released, or else it stays inside where it hurts you more. How can you get it out without hurting someone else or yourself?

Here are three ideas:

1. You can run around outside.

2. You can take huge, deep breaths while counting to ten or twenty.

3. You can kick a ball around or do any other kind of exercise like walking your dog, shooting baskets, dancing, inline skating, or going to the playground.

Once you release some of the energy that anger produces in your body, you'll feel a little better.

Here's a helpful book on dealing with anger:

 *Don't Rant and Rave on Wednesdays! The Children's Anger-Control Book* by Adolph Moser, Ed.D. (Kansas City, MO: Landmark Editions, 1994). Anger can be powerful and sometimes frightening to experience. This books explains what causes anger and helps you learn how to handle and control your anger and frustration in healthy, positive ways.

One other thing that releases anger, stress, or frustration is tears. Crying helps you feel better by letting out the feelings inside you. Crying is also good to do when you're sad. You can cry in private or out in the open. You can cry in front of your mom or dad, or someone else you love. You can cry if you're a girl or a boy. You can cry no matter what age you are. Letting out your tears helps you feel better.

Sometimes, people think that showing feelings isn't okay. That's not true. Emotions are a part of us. They help us to express what's in our head and in our heart. An important part of growing up is accepting your feelings. Don't be afraid to let them show.

You may find it helpful to just sit down and feel the emotions you have inside. Sit quietly and let the feelings wash over you, whether you're angry, scared, sad, lonely, or hurting. For example, if you're feeling frightened, take a deep breath and just let yourself feel frightened—instead of pushing the feeling deeper inside. Next, let that deep breath out and imagine you're sending the scared feelings out of your body and into the air. Do this as many times as you need to.

When you're going through a hard time like this, you might even start to feel numb. This means you don't seem to feel anything at all—like your feelings have switched to "off." Usually, it's a sign you're feeling so much that you're overloaded. Your feelings are buried way deep inside, but they *need* to come out.

Lots of kids—and adults—have found that drawing or writing about their feelings is helpful. Maybe you have a journal or diary. You can use it to describe what you're feeling at any time. (If you want to keep it private, that's okay. You can hide it in a drawer, so no one takes a peek.)

You can also draw or paint pictures that help you get out your emotions. Choose colors that match your mood, or draw fast and hard when you need to release strong emotions. You can play some music that helps you feel a certain way. Loud music can rev you up, while soft music can help you calm down.

You can also find ways to cheer yourself up. Maybe you can read a funny book, look at the comics section of the newspaper, go to a movie, or ask your dad or mom to rent a comedy video for you. You might go to the library for a joke book or call a friend who makes you laugh. Laughing is another healthy way to release feelings and get your mind off of what's bothering you.

All of these activities can help you set your feelings free. Once they're out, it's easier to open up to other people. Opening up means talking, another healthy way to deal with feelings. (See pages 32–38 for more about that.)

At times, you may have another feeling—one that surprises you. You may be relieved, or almost happy, that your parents are getting a divorce. Sometimes, parents argue so often or are so tense that the divorce comes as a relief. In some families, one parent may have really tough problems that affect everyone else—making it seem as if the best thing is for that parent to be away from the rest of the family.

"Some parents make life easier when they get a divorce because if they kept living together in the same house, they'd probably be fighting a lot. And that's harder for everyone—especially the kids."

BOY, 12

This type of situation may be true in your family. If so, you might feel relieved that the divorce is happening. After that, you might feel bad or guilty for thinking that way. It's *okay* to feel relief. It's okay to think the divorce might actually be a good thing. It's okay to look forward to a different way of life.

The most important thing to know is that *any* emotion you feel is okay. Your feelings aren't "good" or "bad"—they just are.

Remember that a divorce can feel like a big storm. Before the storm, the air may be filled with tension. Afterward, the air clears again and the weather eventually returns to normal. In other words, storms don't last forever—and neither do divorces or strong emotions. As time passes, you'll begin to feel like yourself again.

Take a look at these books for more help:

Dear Mr. Henshaw by Beverly Cleary (New York: Harper-Collins, 1994). This story is written as a series of letters and diary entries addressed to a young boy's favorite author. In his letters, ten-year-old Leigh reveals his problems coping with his parents' divorce, being the new boy in school, and finding his own place in the world.

My Parents Are Divorced, Too: A Book for Kids by Kids by Melanie, Annie, and Steven Ford as told to Jan Blackstone-Ford (Washington, DC: Magination Press, 1998). Young authors write about their own experiences with their parents' divorce in a way that can help you understand what you're going through. You'll discover you're not the only one going through such tough problems and changes.

Stress Can Really Get on Your Nerves! by Trevor Romain and Elizabeth Verdick (Minneapolis: Free Spirit Publishing Inc., 2000). If you're feeling worried or anxious—like many kids whose parents are divorcing—this book can help. You'll find out what stress is, how it affects your body and mind, and what you can do about it.

If I need to talk about my feelings, what can I do?

Divorce is a big change that affects your whole life. That's why it's so important to talk about what's going on. Whenever you feel angry, sad, upset, confused, or any other emotion, talk to somebody. That person can be your mom or dad, a relative (grandmother, grandfather, uncle, aunt), or a family friend. If your family attends a place of worship, you could talk to an adult there, like a teacher, youth leader, minister, rabbi, or priest. Find someone you trust who's a good listener. You don't have to go through this alone.

Your parents or a judge may want you to talk to a counselor, social worker, or therapist (experts who help people get through difficult times). You may see this person alone or with other members of your family at a private office or at the courthouse. You may go once or many times, and your parents may see this expert on their own, too. The idea is to talk about how you feel. A conversation with an expert can be helpful, if you say what's really on your mind. Even though it may be hard to tell someone you don't know well about your feelings, it helps. Counselors, social workers, and therapists have lots of ideas about handling feelings and problems.

It also helps to talk to people at school: a teacher or your principal, for example. Find out if there's a school counselor or guidance counselor available. All of these adults can offer advice and help you cope with your feelings.

"I talked to my school counselor. It was good to get it all out, because it's hard for me to talk to people about feelings. If it's sometimes hard for you to talk to people about feelings, you might think it's hard to talk to a counselor—but it's easier than you think."

BOY, 12

How do you start a conversation about your feelings? Here are examples of what you might say:

"My parents are divorcing. Sometimes, I feel scared about it. Can you help me?"

"I feel sad, and I need to talk to someone. Do you have time to talk with me?"

"Sometimes, I get so mad about what's happening. What can I do about my feelings?"

"Is there a support group at school for kids whose parents are getting divorced?"

Do you ever feel as if you need to hide what's going on—that your friends and classmates just wouldn't care or under-stand? Some kids whose parents are divorcing feel this way. They believe the divorce makes them "different" or shows that something's "wrong" with their family. At times, you may feel that the divorce sets you apart from the other kids. You may think that no one else is having problems like this. Actually, some of the kids in your class probably have divorced parents, too. You could talk with them about what it's like to deal with a divorce.

> "I know that other kids' parents are divorced. And kids whose parents aren't divorced still treat me the same as if my parents were together."
>
> **BOY, 12**

Remember that your friends care about you. They're the people you trust. If you try to hide your feelings, your friends may still know something's upsetting you. They may wonder if you're okay. It helps to tell your friends about the divorce.

Here are some words you can say:

> "My parents aren't going to stay married anymore. They're getting a divorce, and I feel upset."

> "My parents are breaking up. That's why I've been stressed out and sad."

> "I feel scared and lonely sometimes. I'm glad to have you as a friend. It helps to talk about it."

You also can talk to your siblings. If you have older sisters or brothers, they may be able to give you advice about handling your feelings. If you and your siblings are close in age, you may find it helpful to talk about what you're going through—after all, who could relate better than the people in your own family? If you have a younger brother or sister, you may be able to help him or her understand what's happening. Just spending time with your siblings is comforting. You can do the things you always do: play outside, play games, watch movies, do puzzles, tell jokes, or just hang out.

Remember, you don't have to go through this alone. Find people to talk to, even if you feel a little shy or embarrassed at first. Once you start talking, the conversations will get easier—and they'll help you feel better.

"Sometimes, I talked to my cat. And even though he couldn't talk back, it felt good to talk to somebody. Besides, a cat can't make any judgments about you or your family."

BOY, 10

What if my parents are mad or upset?

Different families deal with divorce in different ways. Some parents are able to keep a friendly relationship during and after a divorce. Other parents argue or may hardly speak to each other. No matter what the situation between them is like, your mom and dad will probably seem more angry, tense, upset, or sad these days. Divorce is hard on everyone, even on the adults who decide to get the divorce in the first place!

You might notice more tension in your home. As a result, you may feel angry or pressured. You may feel that your dad or mom has made your life much more difficult. What can you do? Take a look at pages 21–31 for suggestions on dealing with strong feelings like anger. After you've found healthy ways to handle your feelings, talk about them with someone you trust.

Sometimes, it's best to talk directly to your mom or dad. You may feel uncomfortable about doing this, especially if part of you thinks your dad or mom caused the problem. For example, suppose you're mad at your mom because she yells at your dad. What's the best thing to do? You've got a few choices.

You might decide to talk with her face-to-face. You could say, "Mom, I'm feeling angry that you yell at Dad so much." If talking to her isn't possible, for whatever reason, you might want to write her a letter or an email message. If you do this, share your feelings without placing blame. Always try to treat a person you're angry with in a respectful way. Why? Because if you do, you'll be better able to work things out between you.

If your mom isn't available, you might decide to go to your dad. You could say, "Dad, I'm mad that Mom yells at you a lot." Your dad may be able to help you with your feelings. Another option is to tell someone else how you feel—an adult you trust, an older sibling or cousin, or a counselor. You could then ask that person for some advice on handling your feelings.

Sometimes, you might be worried about your parents, especially if you often see them angry or sad. You may even see your mom or dad cry, which can be pretty scary or upsetting. You probably remember times when you cried and felt better afterward. Parents will feel better faster if they cry.

"When I see my mom cry, I give her hugs. I sometimes try to make her laugh with a funny face. She always says she will be fine and that she is just sad."

BOY, 10

You may think you need to take care of your dad or mom during this difficult time. For example, you might believe that it's now your job to try to keep the peace or take care of things around the home. It's not, though. Grown-ups are supposed to take care of children, not the other way around.

But you can help in little ways:

1. Give hugs.
2. Say "I love you" often.
3. Write notes or draw pictures that show you care.
4. Bring a box of tissues if your mom or dad is crying.
5. Tell a relative or family friend what's going on at home. Ask for some help.

Your dad and mom need time to heal, and so do you. Even though it may be hard to accept, healing takes time.

Here's a good story about dealing with the fighting that often goes along with divorce:

It's Not the End of the World by Judy Blume (New York: Yearling Books, 1986). Karen has decided she'll never get married because all her parents do is fight, and now they're talking about divorce. At first Karen is sure they can work it out if they try, but after meeting a friend whose parents are also divorced, she starts to rethink whether her parents should stay together.

Who will take care of me?

Your parents' divorce probably means that you won't get to see your mom or dad as often as you did before. For example, when you're at your mom's home, she may not spend as much time with you, especially if she now has a new job or is working longer hours. The same goes for your dad. Your parents will have new responsibilities after the divorce, but they still love you and will take care of you.

As your parents go through their divorce (and afterward, too), they'll need to make decisions about how to care for you and your sisters or brothers, if you have any. Some of these decisions will be about your schedule. Others will be about money.

Often, one parent pays *child support* to the other parent. Child support money helps pay for things you need as you grow up. In some divorce cases, one parent pays *alimony* to the other parent. Alimony is money that helps your mom or dad with bills, school, or other needs.

You might be worried that you won't have enough money, food, or clothing now that your family lives in two places. If you're anxious about this, talk to one or both of your parents. Don't keep scary questions like this bottled up inside you.

You might say:

"Dad, I feel worried. Will we be okay?"

"Mom, are we going to have enough food and clothes now?"

"Sometimes, I'm scared there won't be enough money for the things we need. Can you help me understand what's happening?"

It's true that divorce affects a family's money situation. Neither your dad nor your mom will have as much money as before. You may notice that your parents seem worried about money. They may sometimes tell you, "We can't afford that right now." If this happens, you may be disappointed or angry. Instead of thinking about what you don't have or can't have, think about what you do have. When you focus on the good things in your life, you'll feel more positive inside. Feeling positive—looking on the bright side—helps you get through a bad day or a rough spot.

"My mom was worried that we couldn't afford the new townhouse. I offered her my allowance to help. She said that it was my money, and she would take care of the townhouse. I was just trying to help because she says we can't afford everything that we could before."

BOY, 8

On the other hand, one or both of your parents may buy you extra presents, hoping this will make you feel better. One of your parents may even get you a big, fancy gift to try to make you like him or her more than the other parent. Deep inside, parents know that trying to "buy" love in this way isn't okay. They probably realize that being a parent isn't a popularity contest. But during or after a divorce, many parents feel guilty and confused. They may do things they wouldn't usually do.

Your mom and dad are doing their best to take care of you. If you don't feel secure for some reason, talk to another adult you trust. Lots of people can help: relatives, the parents of your best friends, teachers, social workers, or school counselors.

Because of the divorce, you'll probably have a schedule that divides up the time you spend with each parent. This can be confusing, especially at first. A good way to keep track of where you need to be is by using a calendar. You can mark which days you'll be with your dad and which days you'll be with your mom. Calendars are also helpful tools for planning what you'll be doing on holidays, birthdays, and other special occasions. (For more about these events, see pages 63–66.) You may want to keep a calendar at your mom's and at your dad's. Hang the calendars in a central place, such as on the refrigerator or on a bulletin board.

"I was so relieved when my mom and dad agreed on how to divide the time they spend with my brother and me. I see each of them every week. When I start to miss my mom, it's time to go back to her place. When I start to miss my dad, it's time to be with him again."

BOY, 8

Your schedule with your parents may change as you get older. Your dad or mom may ask you how your schedule is working and what changes you want to make. On the other hand, your parents may decide on a new schedule without your help. As grown-ups, they're in charge of your schedule until you're an adult. If you have concerns about your schedule, speak up. See if your parents can find ways to make things easier for you.

If you're online, check out these helpful Web sites any time:

KidsHealth
www.kidshealth.org
KidsHealth is one of the largest sites on the Web providing doctor-approved health information about children. Do a search for "divorce" to find several articles marked especially for kids, teens, or parents about moving, dealing with divorce, surviving stepsiblings, managing the holidays with two families, and many other divorce-related topics.

Kids' Turn
www.kidsturn.org
Kids' Turn is a program that helps kids learn and feel better about divorce. Read how other kids feel about it, play games and activities, look at artwork and articles for and by kids whose parents are divorced, and check out the huge list of books that deal with divorce. Kids' Turn also has a section for parents and experts.

Where will I live?

Sometimes, a divorce means that a family has to sell their house or move to a different townhouse or apartment. When parents have less money, they may move to a smaller place and sell some of their belongings. This can be really hard for parents and their kids to face. It's difficult to say good-bye to a familiar home, especially during a tough time.

If you're moving, talk about your feelings and any fears you may have. You can write in your journal or diary, too. You'll also feel better if you get some exercise and spend time with your friends.

Here are some other resources that can help if you're moving:

A New Room for William by Sally Grindley, illustrated by Carol Thompsen (Cambridge, MA: Candlewick Press, 2000). In this story, a young boy named William and his mother move to a new place. At first, William doesn't have any friends or like his new room. Find out how William finally learns to adjust to his new home.

Good-bye, House: A Kids' Guide to Moving by Ann Banks and Nancy Evans (New York: Crown Publishing Group, 1999). This guide and activity book is designed to help you handle all the changes that occur when you're moving to a new home. Tips and activities help you organize your stuff for the move, adjust to your new home and neighborhood, survive your first day at a new school, keep in touch with your old friends, and a lot more. Also includes stickers you can use to label your boxes during the move.

Let's Make a Move! A Creative Visualization Book for Children by Beverly D. Roman (Wilmington, NC: BR Anchor Publications, 2000). This book offers activities to help make your move a smooth transition, plus Internet resources that provide more information. Calendar stickers and box labels are included.

Your parents' divorce probably means you won't get to see your mom or dad as often as you did before. It may also mean that when you're with each parent, you won't have as much time together anymore. For example, maybe only one of your parents had a job before the divorce but now both do. Or maybe one parent now has two jobs or works extra hours to make more money. Maybe your dad or mom has gone back to school. If your parents have added responsibilities like these, they'll be busier than usual. You may spend more time in after-school care or with baby-sitters.

These changes can bring with them feelings of loneliness and frustration. If this is how you feel, talk about it. Perhaps your mom or dad can arrange to spend extra time with you. Maybe a relative you're close to can come for a visit. Find different ways of staying close to your parents and other family members: talk on the phone or send letters and emails, for example.

Other things will probably be different in your two homes as well. You may have your own room for the first time, or you may now share a room with siblings. You may have certain clothes or belongings that you keep at each home or pack to take with you. Keep toothbrushes, shampoo, pajamas, and stuff like that in both of your homes so you'll have less to take back and forth.

"If you get gifts for a birthday or holiday, you might want to keep all of them in the home you spend the most time in. But it makes each home more fun when you have special things at each one. I think it's better to keep some of your favorite stuff at both homes."

BOY, 10

Remember that life is changing for your dad and mom, too. They have to get used to your new schedule and to additional responsibilities. One or both of your parents may be adjusting to cooking new foods, balancing a tighter budget, or taking care of chores like laundry or household repairs. You could offer to help, so these duties won't take as long—and so you can spend more time with your mom or dad.

"In our home before the divorce, it was my mom who did the cooking. So when I went to my dad's new house, the food was different. I learned that you have to be willing to try new things but also to be honest about what you like."

GIRL, 8

When your parents start living in two places, your life will change. You may miss the old days when your family lived in the same place. After everyone in your family is used to this new way of life, you'll feel better. It's not easy to adjust to a new home, a new schedule, and a new way of life—but you can do it. Lots of kids have.

"Now that my mom and dad are separated, it's easier to fall asleep. They aren't keeping me awake with their fighting anymore."

BOY, 10

"If your parents are getting divorced, you have to keep your spirits up. Even though there might be problems, things will always turn out for the better in the future."

BOY, 12

What is it like to have two homes?

Having two homes instead of one will mean changes. Still, some things will stay the same. For example, you might still go to the same school or have some of the same after-school activities.

"Something that is good about living in two different homes is you get two of everything. That's what I enjoy about it."

GIRL, 8

"You're probably going to find that a lot of the things you're going to miss at each home are things you get to do anyway, just at a different place. And also, I didn't know that my mom could be so much fun, until my dad moved out. I think both of my parents are better parents now."

BOY, 12

Many kids have discovered that there are good things and bad things about having two homes. At first, you'll probably spend a lot of time getting used to each new place. Many kids with two homes have found that it's helpful to have routines they can rely on at each place. You may find that this helps you, too.

For example, getting up and going to bed at the same time in each home helps you adjust to being in a new place. You may also want to make a special area for doing homework—a desk or table that you always use, for example. Even though it's sometimes confusing to go from one home to another, you still have to get your schoolwork done. It can help to have a dependable place to do it.

You can also keep special reminders of your other home and your other parent with you, if you'd like. When you're at your mom's home, you may want to put a photo of your dad on a dresser or on the wall. At your dad's, you may want to have special things your mom gave you, such as a toy, a note, or a picture. These keepsakes can help you feel closer to your other parent.

One major difference between your two homes may be the rules you have to follow. Before the divorce, your parents worked together to make the rules about homework, when friends could come over, manners, and other important things. Now that your parents live apart, the rules at their two homes may be different. (For example, your bedtime might be earlier at your dad's, or your mom may have a special rule about the kind of snacks you're allowed to eat.) It's confusing when the rules and expectations in one home are different than they are in the other home.

As parents, your dad and mom make the rules. As their child, you have to do what they tell you. Sometimes, this may not seem fair. If you're confused about the rules, let your mom and dad know. If you think a rule should be changed, bring it up in a calm, kind way.

You might say:

"Dad, I'm wondering if we can change the rule about homework time. Your rule is that we start homework right after school, but I'd like to have an hour to get outside and play first. Then I'll have more energy when I start my homework. Can we work something out?"

"Mom, I'd like to be able to call Dad after school each day. It's important for me to talk to him. Can we make a rule about calling at a certain time? I'd really like that."

This approach is better than yelling, complaining, or whining about a rule—guaranteed! Your parents will be more likely to listen to you and consider your feelings if you talk to them calmly and have good reasons for changing a rule. You may be tempted to say something like, "I don't have to do that at Mom's" or "Dad lets me do this at his place," but that approach doesn't work. Stop and take a deep breath instead. Remember that grown-ups are in charge of the rules in their own homes.

"Now I'm used to the rules in my two homes. I learned that rules can be fair, even if they're different."

BOY, 10

What about birthdays and holidays?

Birthdays, holidays, and other special occasions will be different now. Your parents will probably have a schedule for you on these special days. For example, one year you may be with your mom for Hanukkah, and the following year you'll be with your dad. You might spend Christmas Eve with one parent and Christmas day with the other parent. Some families celebrate holidays and birthdays twice, on two different days.

Holidays and other special days are emotional times for everyone, especially in divorced families. You and your parents may feel sad not to be together on these important days. You may wish your parents would get back together. (For more about this, see pages 99–101.) You may be excited to be with one parent but miss the other parent at the same time. You may worry about what your mom or dad will do without you when you're not there. You may not have as much fun because some of your family's traditions have changed. Lots of kids feel these ways.

"My hardest thing was Father's Day. I felt lonely for my dad. My mom helped me make and send a card, and that made me feel a little better. Talking to my dad on the phone helped, too."

GIRL, 7

What can you do to make these times easier for yourself? Instead of focusing on what's "missing" or what's different, think of ways to keep special days special. For example, remind your dad or mom about the parts of each holiday you love most. Maybe you enjoy picking out gifts, helping to decorate your home, making cards, singing special songs, going to your place of worship, or eating a particular meal. Think of ways to keep these traditions going.

Make new traditions, too. Is there something you'd like to change about how the holidays are celebrated? Now is a good time to let your parents know. You can also think of something special to do for someone else, such as donating a toy to a child in need. Bringing joy into someone else's life brings joy into your own.

"You might celebrate holidays in a different way than you're used to. This can be good because different experiences can be good. Usually at my dad's home we go out to eat for birthdays, and it's fun because we each get to choose where we want to go. At my mom's, we celebrate at home and we get to choose what we want to eat. That's fun, too. I like having different ways to celebrate."

GIRL, 8

Now you may actually get to celebrate some holidays twice. You probably never had two birthday parties before or celebrated Thanksgiving twice, and now you will. You may get to go on two summer-vacation trips instead of one.

Holidays and special occasions are times to remember what's good and what's worth celebrating in your life. You have people who love you, friends you care about (and who care about you), and many other blessings. When you remind yourself about the good things in your life, you'll realize you have a lot to look forward to each day of the year.

If you need help thinking of things to celebrate, take a look at this book:

I'm in Charge of Celebrations by Byrd Baylor and Peter Parnall (New York: Charles Scribner's Sons, 1986). In this story, a girl who lives in the desert creates her own special holidays and celebrations almost every day of the year, just by noticing the world around her.

What if I miss my mom or dad?

On some days or evenings, you'll be with your dad and not see your mom. On some days or evenings, you'll be with your mom and not see your dad. Your schedule may leave you feeling a mix of emotions—sad, happy, frustrated, unsure—all at the same time.

It's hard to handle so many feelings. You may miss the days when your family lived in one place. When you haven't seen your mom for a while, you'll feel excited to be with her. At the same time, you may wish you didn't have to say good-bye to your dad. These hellos and good-byes can be sad, confusing, and stressful.

When it's time to leave one parent and see the other (transition times), you may feel upset. Being a kid in a divorced family isn't easy, and transition times can be the hardest part. Sometimes, you'll feel that, just as you get settled in one place, it's time to leave for the other. You may cry or get angry. You may not want to go to your other home—or you may say you don't feel like going, even if you really want to see your other parent. At times, you'll feel sorry for the parent you're leaving. Lots of kids feel this way. It takes time for everyone to adjust to these transitions.

If your mom and dad have arranged a schedule where you don't get to see one of them for a very long time, you may feel especially sad or confused. You may worry about what your other parent is doing when he or she isn't with you. You may wonder if your dad or mom will forget about you when you aren't there. You may wonder if he or she is doing okay. These thoughts and worries are normal.

Going back and forth between two homes can be difficult. It's sad having to say good-bye to one parent. You may also feel upset to leave behind pets, favorite books or toys, or other things that are special to you. Even if a part of you is sad, another part will probably feel happy to see your other parent (and that parent will be happy, too). You may also feel excited to visit your other home.

"I had to get used to the fact that my dad wasn't around to play with me all the time. But now it's easier because I do get to see my dad quite a bit. We act silly, play games, and even go on trips."

GIRL, 8

It's okay to miss your dad or mom (or your belongings) wherever you are. Thinking about someone you love and missing that person is part of being human. You don't have to hide these feelings.

It may help to remember that you can stay in touch with your other parent in different ways. Perhaps you can call at a certain time each day or night. You might write letters or make a card. You might send an email message. There are lots of ways to stay close when someone you love isn't right there beside you.

One other thing you can do is write about or draw your feelings. If you have a journal or art supplies, bring them with you when you visit your other parent. Expressing yourself by writing or drawing can help you feel better. You could show your mom or dad what you've written, if you want to. (That's up to you.) The two of you could draw pictures together, too. Playing or listening to music can also help you feel better.

"You might feel lonely when your parents first get a divorce. And you might feel lonely for a long time after, too. But it *does* get better. Things will be okay."

GIRL, 8

"When I would get really frustrated about having to go back and forth between my parents, I would go to my room, turn on my favorite songs, and just listen to music."

GIRL, 9

What if I don't miss my mom or dad?

Some kids may feel relieved to be away from a parent who was hurting them in some way. Maybe before or during the divorce, the parent got angry a lot and yelled or hit. Or maybe the parent had a problem with drinking alcohol, doing drugs, or gambling money. This happens in some families. Maybe it has happened in yours.

Depending on the arrangements made during the divorce, you may now spend much more time with one of your parents than the other one. For example, your parents or a judge may have decided that you should live mostly with your mom and see your dad only occasionally. On the other hand, the arrangement may be that you spend most of your time with your dad and only see your mom once in a while. But what if you don't feel like seeing your other parent at all? What happens then?

In divorce cases, adults make the decisions. Sometimes, children are given a chance to talk about their needs, too. In the end, though, the grown-ups decide what kind of custody or visitation arrangements to make. Usually, the adults at the courts (lawyers and judges) decide it's best for the kids to see *both* parents—unless there has been abuse in the family. The courts want each parent to keep a connection with their children.

Sometimes, one of the parents may see their kids under *supervised visitation.* This means that another adult (for example, a family member, counselor, or friend) stays nearby as the mom or dad visits with their children. Perhaps one of your parents has a supervised visitation arrangement. If that's the case, you'll probably have mixed feelings about these visits.

You might feel scared or uncertain. You might feel angry that this parent is still in your life. Even if you aren't in a supervised visitation arrangement, you may have these feelings. For example, your dad or mom may live in a home that's uncomfortable for you, for whatever reason. (Maybe it's dirty, or maybe you're left alone there for long periods of time.) Sometimes, kids don't really miss the other parent much or don't want to go to their other home for visits. You may feel this way at times—maybe even all the time.

This is a difficult situation to be in. You're still a child, and the adults around you are making decisions about your life. You may feel that the decisions are unfair or aren't what's best for you. You may feel scared, alone, angry, or upset about seeing your other parent. You may even feel forced into something that makes you very uncomfortable. If you feel any of these ways, you might get really angry or even try to refuse to see the other parent.

A better choice is to talk about what's really going on. You can talk to your other parent, or you can go to a school counselor, a teacher, a grown-up at your place of worship, or another adult you trust.

If the court decides to give your other parent a chance to be a better parent, it might happen. Maybe your other parent can improve over time. Although it may be hard, people *can* and *do* change for the better. Keep talking to the other important adults in your life. They can give you advice and help you.

If you're being hurt by one (or both) of your parents and you need some help, find an adult you trust and talk about what's happening. You can also contact this hotline:

 Girls and Boys Town National Hotline
1-800-448-3000 (This is a free call.)
www.boystown.org/hotline/crisis.htm

You can call or contact this hotline any time—experts are available twenty-four hours a day. These trained counselors listen and can give you "right now" answers, so you'll know what to do. They'll give advice on topics such as divorce, anger, fear, problems with parents, abuse, and much more.

What if one of my parents doesn't see me anymore?

"I didn't feel like I was important. For a while after my dad left, I kept thinking he would come back. I kept getting my hopes up over and over. Then later I knew it wouldn't happen. Talking to people about it helped."

GIRL, 10

In some divorces, one parent may leave and not stay in touch anymore or hardly at all. Maybe this is happening in your family. If it is, there are some important things you need to know.

First and most important: *it's not your fault this happened.* Nothing you ever did, said, or thought made one parent decide to go away. Sometimes, grown-ups have serious problems they don't know how to fix. They believe that getting away may be an answer. Sometimes, adults get so swept up in their own troubles that they don't know what to do. When this happens, they may forget how wonderful their children are and how much their children need both of their parents.

The second thing you need to know is that you still have a family. One parent may be gone, but the other one isn't. If you're scared, sad, lonely, confused, angry, or upset, tell your other parent.

You might say:

"Why did Mom leave?"

"I'm scared that Dad will never come back. What can I do?"

"I miss Mom, but I'm angry with her. How can I handle it?"

"I wish Dad would come back. What can I do?"

"Dad, I get scared you're going to leave, too."

You might ask to talk to an expert like a counselor, social worker, or therapist. Your school may have a counselor who helps students work through problems, but if no one like this is available, ask your mom or dad about seeing an expert outside of school. If you attend a place of worship, another option is to get some guidance from a leader there.

At a time like this, you need love and understanding from other people in your life. It's okay to reach out to adults you know, especially if you're feeling that you've been left behind by someone you love. You may think that you're a "terrible kid" because one of your parents isn't there for you anymore—but it's *not* true. Nothing you did caused your parent to leave.

Getting support from other adults and your friends is one of the best ways you can help yourself right now. Telling yourself you're not to blame is another good way to cope.

Here are some things you can do if you're feeling lonely or down:

1. Talk to friends in person or by phone.

2. Call your aunt or uncle, or another relative.

3. Send an email or write a letter to someone you care about.

4. Watch a favorite movie—one that makes you laugh.

5. Hang out with your brother or sister.

6. Invite someone over.

7. Volunteer your time helping someone in need.

8. Pet your dog or cat, visit with your hamster or bird, or watch your fish swim around.

9. Hug a pillow or favorite stuffed animal.

10. Hug somebody.

What if I feel "stuck in the middle"?

Once your parents start living in two places, life for your family will change. Many of these changes will be strange and difficult. Later on, after everyone in your family is used to your new way of life, you'll begin to feel better. Maybe you're starting to feel better already.

The hardest times might be when you're going back and forth between your parents' two homes. Many kids feel like they're being torn in half. They like to carry special belongings—a favorite game or activity, family photos, a stuffed animal, a special blanket, or a journal—to each home. Your special things can make you more comfortable, no matter where you are.

As you go back and forth between your dad's and your mom's homes, there may be some tension—maybe even a lot of tension. For example, some moms and dads who are divorcing or are already divorced are angry at each other. They may get mad at each other in front of you.

It's hard to be in the middle of two people who are fighting. Sometimes, your dad and mom may argue in front of you, cry, say mean words, or give each other dirty looks. At other times, your parents might refuse to speak to each other.

"Sometimes I just felt like I was being torn. I didn't like it at all. Even if what my dad said about my mom was true, it made me feel bad to hear it."

BOY, 11

How can you handle these situations? You can tell your mom and dad that their arguments or behaviors upset you. In a calm voice, let them know that you're scared or stressed out (or whatever you're feeling). Usually, parents will stop fighting, at least in front of you, if they know they're upsetting you. If they don't stop, you may need to leave the room for a while until things settle down.

If your parents have a disagreement, it's about grown-up stuff. You don't have to get involved—and it's better not to. Don't try to get in the middle. This is something your parents need to work out between themselves.

It's normal for parents to have disagreements. Your parents might disagree or argue about lots of things. You don't have to take sides. Their arguments are theirs, not yours. No matter what the argument is about, it's *not* your fault. You didn't cause it or start it. You're *not* responsible for it.

If you get stressed out, here are some things you can do:

1. Call a friend.
2. Listen to music.
3. Play a game, do art, dance, or practice your jump shot.
4. Write your feelings in a journal or diary.
5. Get some exercise: jump rope, take a walk, or ride your bike.

When adults go through a divorce, they may get caught up in their own feelings at times. They may forget that their kids still need to love both their mom and their dad. They may act in ways that make their kids feel as if they're stuck in the middle. They may even say negative things behind each other's backs. As a result, their kids may feel miserable or confused.

What can you do if this often happens to you? Understand that dads and moms make mistakes, just like any other grown-up (or kid). Remind them that it's okay for you to love both parents—and that you don't want to choose sides. And remind yourself of this often, as well. It's okay to love your mom and your dad now and forever. You have plenty of love for both of your parents, and they have plenty for you.

Here are some words you can say if you feel caught in the middle:

"Mom, it's okay for me to love Dad. I love you, too."

"Dad, I still love Mom and I always will."

"Mom and Dad, I feel scared when you argue in front of me. Please stop."

"I don't have to pick sides."

"I feel upset. Please don't put me in the middle of things."

"I will always love you both, and nothing can change that."

After time goes by, your parents will learn to be more polite to each other. Then they'll be more likely to remember that they share something very important: you. If your parents are putting you in the middle, be patient and continue talking to other people you trust. Keep reminding your parents how much you need to love them both.

What about my grandparents?

Lots of kids whose parents are divorcing wonder what will happen with their grandparents. If you have grandparents, they'll still be your grandparents. (The same goes for your other relatives—you'll still have them, too.)

The good news is that, in most cases, your grandparents will still be able to visit you, talk to you, and take you places. You're still their grandchild, and the special feelings they have for you won't change. They'll love you as much as they ever did!

One kind of change might happen, though, and that's how your grandparents feel about your mom or dad. Sometimes, for example, your dad's parents might be angry with your mom because of the divorce. Your mom's parents might be angry with your dad. On the other hand, both sets of grandparents might be upset with both of your parents. Grown-ups have lots of painful feelings during divorce, just like kids do.

Your grandparents may not hide their angry feelings from you. They may express that they're disappointed, sad, or upset. They can't help these feelings. They probably thought your parents would always be together. Plus, your grandparents will be concerned about how the divorce will affect you. They may blame your mom or dad (or both of them) for what's going on—even though blame doesn't help anyone.

Another thing that might happen is that your mom may not feel as comfortable around your dad's parents, or your dad may not feel as comfortable around your mom's parents (or the other way around, too). Divorces can make life very complicated. When grown-ups feel upset or uncomfortable, it may be harder for them to see each other. They may forget that you still want to be close to all of your grandparents and that you still want to visit, write letters, or talk.

You can remind everyone how you feel by saying words like these:

"Dad, let's spend time with Grandma. I miss her."

"Mom, I really miss Granddad and Grammy.
When can I call or write to them?"

"Grandpa, when you say bad things about Mom, I feel upset."

"Please don't talk that way about my dad, Grandma."

"I still love everyone in my family. Don't forget that."

"I need Mom and Dad both, even though they're divorcing.
Please remember that."

"I need my grandparents, even though you're getting divorced.
Please remember that."

Over time, your grandparents may come to accept the divorce, just like you will. Until then, all you need to do is remember that your grandparents still love you. You can love them and enjoy having them in your life, even if the grown-ups are feeling uncomfortable or tense.

"I guess me and my brothers are lucky because everything with our grandparents is the same. We still see them, and they act the same. And sometimes my mom even takes us on a road trip to my dad's parents' home to visit them and other relatives. We're lucky that everyone gets along."

GIRL, 8

If you don't see your grandparents as often now or if they live far away from you, here are some ways to stay in touch:

1. Send email or write letters.

2. Draw pictures to mail.

3. Call and talk to them on the phone.

4. Mail a card on Grandparents' Day.

5. Send photos of yourself.

What if my parents are keeping secrets from each other?

One of your parents might tell you something, and then ask you to keep it a secret from your other parent. For example, your mom might say, "Don't tell Dad we're going on a trip." Your dad might say, "Mom can't know that I bought you this." You might feel confused or upset if you're asked to keep secrets. Keeping secrets isn't easy. You might think your mom or dad has a right to know something. Or you might feel guilty if you accidentally let a secret slip out.

"Keeping secrets sometimes feels like lying. In a way, it's kind of like lying. It makes me feel stressed."

GIRL, 10

This is a difficult part of being divorced for grown-ups—and it's hard on their children, too. After a divorce, your dad and mom have separate homes and separate lives. You're still a part of their lives, and in this way, your parents stay connected. Still, they want their privacy. Your dad won't want your mom to know everything that he's doing, and the same goes for your mom. Your mom may not care about everything that happens in your other home, and the same is true for your dad.

You may get mixed signals from your parents. On the one hand, they may ask you to keep certain things private. On the other hand, they may ask you personal questions about what goes on in your other home. This is confusing!

What should you do? The best solution is not to keep secrets, especially ones that make you uncomfortable. You should be able to tell your mom about what goes on in your dad's home, and you should be able to tell your dad about what goes on in your mom's home. If your parents ask you to keep secrets, let them know this upsets you.

You might say:

"Dad, I get upset when you tell me Mom
can't know certain things."

"Mom, please don't ask me not to tell Dad about this."

"I hope I can tell you what happens at Mom's. That's my other
home, and I want to share what goes on there."

"Keeping secrets like this is hard for me, Mom.
Please don't ask me to keep this a secret."

"I like to be able to tell both of you the truth."

If this doesn't help, you may need to speak to someone outside of your family: a teacher, a school counselor, a grown-up at your place of worship, your principal, or someone else you trust. Let this person know what's happening in your two homes—especially if one parent is asking you to keep secrets about things that make you really uncomfortable or upset.

If you're keeping a secret about something very difficult that's happening at home and you need to talk to someone right away, see page 77 for information on the Girls and Boys Town National Hotline, a place you can call (for free) or reach online immediately.

Secrets can hurt. They can leave you confused or make you feel unsafe. If this is how you feel, let the secrets out. You'll feel better if you do.

What if I feel like a messenger?

During or after a divorce, your parents might have trouble speaking to each other politely—or at all. You love your parents, and when you love people, it's hard to see them treat each other badly.

If your parents act angry with each other or refuse to talk to each other, you may feel caught in the middle. (Read more about this on pages 82–86.) At times, you may feel like a messenger who has to carry messages back and forth between your parents. For instance, your dad may ask you to tell your mom you need permission to go on a field trip. Your mom may ask you to give your dad some other message from your school. No big deal, right? Actually, these kinds of messages *can* be a big deal. What if you forget to tell your mom or dad? Then you might feel as if you're in trouble or have done something wrong. In the process, the message gets lost.

Your parents will have lots of things to communicate about while you're growing up. They need to make decisions about what's happening with school, your after-school care or activities, holidays or special events, doctor or dentist appointments, travel arrangements, and other important things. Part of their job as parents is to take care of you, so they'll talk to each other or communicate by mail or email.

Your parents may sometimes forget that your job isn't to carry messages back and forth. If so, you can remind them.

You might say:

> "Dad, can you please mail this letter to
> Mom instead of asking me to deliver it?"

> "Mom, it would be better for you to tell Dad yourself."

> "I might not remember the message.
> Please take care of it yourself."

> "When you ask me to do these things, I feel like
> a messenger. Please don't ask me anymore."

If you feel anxious about saying something like this to your mom or dad, you can talk to another grown-up that you trust. Explain what's happening and how you feel. If possible, see if that person would be willing to remind your parents that you're not a messenger.

Will my parents ever get back together?

Lots of kids like to think about their dad and mom getting back together. It can be comforting to imagine everybody living together in one place again. The truth is, there's nothing you can do to make this happen. Almost always, a divorce means your parents will never live together again.

This isn't easy to accept. It's a normal feeling to want your parents to get back together again (it's also a normal feeling not to want this). Some kids may try anything to help their parents make up or love each other like they once did. For example, some kids beg their parents to stay together and say things like, "Mom says she can't live without you" or "Dad always talks about how much he misses you" (even if no one really said these things). Some kids pretend to be sick, so their parents will worry about them and maybe get back together. Even if you're tempted to do these things, it's best not to. Instead, focus your energy on dealing with the divorce and coping with the changes in your life. You'll feel better if you try to move forward, rather than always looking back.

It may help to talk to your friends or classmates whose parents are divorced. They probably wished their parents would stay together or get back together, too. Maybe your friends will explain that, once they got over these feelings, they realized the divorce was better for their family in the long run. Often, parents who divorce feel happier once the marriage is over, and they become better parents.

Your parents have decided that the divorce was the solution for their problems. You may see them feeling sad, angry, or lonely, but the solution isn't for them to get back together. They need time to work through their painful feelings. They need time to adjust to their decision. You need time, too.

If you'd like to read a story about this, here's one to check out:

Don't Make Me Smile by Barbara Park (Marco, FL: Bancroft-Sage Publishing Inc., 1999). Charlie's parents have just told him they're getting a divorce—and they expect him to be *happy* for them! Instead of being cheerful, he decides to show them how bad he really feels about it. Read about how Charlie copes and the lessons he learns from his not-so-helpful behaviors.

What if my dad or mom starts dating?

During or after a divorce, your mom or dad (or both of them) may start dating other people. This may come as a big surprise to you. You might not like seeing—or even thinking about—your mom or dad with someone new.

This is even worse if you're still wishing your parents would get back together. You may see this new person as a threat—someone who's trying to replace your mom or dad. You may be stressed, angry, or disappointed. It's hard to adjust to the idea of "sharing" your dad or mom with somebody else.

All of these feelings are natural, but they can hurt. One thing you need to know is that if your mom or dad dates someone, this doesn't mean you're "not good enough" or "not special enough." Sometimes, kids feel rejected if one of their parents starts dating again. This isn't a sign of rejection—it's a sign that your parent is ready to make new adult friends and enjoy a new relationship. Your parent still has plenty of love for you! That won't change.

You may feel awkward or confused if your dad or mom introduces you to someone new. If so, ask questions when you have some time alone with that parent.

You might say:

"Dad, why do you want to find someone new?"

"Mom, why are you dating now?"

"Why is this person special to you?"

"Do you still love me?"

"I feel hurt when I see you with him.
How can I handle these feelings?"

"When I see you dating other women,
I feel weird about it. What can I do?"

"I thought we were getting closer, but now I
see you with someone else. I don't like it when
you're with this person."

You may have even more questions like:

"Is my mom going to get remarried now?"

"Is my dad in love with someone new?"

"Is it normal to date lots of people after a divorce?"

"What if I don't like the person my mom or dad is dating?"

"Is this person right for my dad or mom?"

"Is it okay for me to feel that it's too soon for
this to be happening in our family?"

"Is this person my mom or dad is dating going
to be a part of my life now?"

These are good questions, and you need to ask them. Talk to the parent who has started dating again or to another trusted adult.

Here's a book that may help, too:

 *Amber Brown Wants Extra Credit* by Paula Danziger (New York: G.P. Putnam's Sons, 1996). Change is the key word for Amber Brown's life. In the Amber Brown series (which also includes *Amber Brown Sees Red, Amber Brown Is Feeling Blue, Forever Amber Brown*), Amber is a fourth grader who's dealing with her parents' divorce, her best friend moving away, her dad moving to France, her mom getting remarried, her dad moving back to town, and her own feelings of being torn between her parents. Through it all, Amber has to keep a sense of humor and learn that change is a natural part of life.

What's a stepmom or stepdad?

Your parents' marriage may have ended, but it isn't the end of your family. Once you're in a family, you're always in it. Yet, families change and grow. At some point, one or both of your parents may remarry. If a parent does remarry, you'll have a new stepmom or stepdad—and maybe stepbrothers and stepsisters. You may even get new aunts and uncles, cousins, and grandparents, too.

"My mom and dad are still friends, but my dad did marry again."

GIRL, 8

"My stepmom is pretty cool. I still love my mom best, but my stepmom is neat, too."

BOY, 7

Families come in all shapes and sizes. Sometimes, families are small, with just two people, for example. Or they can be big with kids from different marriages and lots and lots of relatives. (Instead of having a family tree, you might have a family forest!) Big families can be fun, and so can small ones. Either way, it's a big adjustment for everyone involved.

If your new stepmom or stepdad has kids of her or his own, you might wonder where you fit in. Maybe in your old family, you used to be the oldest and now you'll be in the middle between new stepbrothers and stepsisters. You may have to share a bedroom with a new brother or sister. Your stepbrothers and stepsisters may have different schedules with their mom or dad. Sometimes, you might all be in the same place at the same time; at other times, you won't be. You might think you need a magic calculator just to figure it all out!

There are so many feelings that go along with a huge change like having a new kind of family: fear, anger, sadness, frustration, loneliness, excitement, hopefulness, confusion, guilt, and anxiety, just to name a few. At times, you may feel as if you don't know who you are anymore or you don't know where you fit in. You may wonder if you'll ever be close to your mom and dad again, especially if they have a new husband or wife or additional kids. You may feel as if your world has turned upside down and you no longer know which way is up.

If this describes you, read some books about divorce, remarriage, blended families, and how all these changes can feel. Here are a few to start with:

Families by Meredith Tax (New York: Feminist Press at The City University of New York, 1996). Six-year-old Angie discovers all the different family combinations that can exist as a result of divorce, remarriage, and single parenting. Travel with Angie as she explores common and unique families and learns that (as she says in the end), "Families are who you live with and who you love."

Let's Talk About It: Stepfamilies by Fred Rogers (New York: Putnam Publishing Group, 1997). If your parents remarry, you'll have lots of changes to adjust to: new rules, new siblings, a new home, a new parent. In clear, simple language, this book helps you learn how to cope with all the changes, so you can find your place in your new family.

My Mother Got Married: And Other Disasters by Barbara Park (New York: Random House, 1990). Charles is finally adjusting to life after his parents' divorce, until his mom decides to remarry. In this sequel to *Don't Make Me Smile*, he has to learn to deal with his mom marrying Ben and having Ben's two children move in with them. Although everyone tells Charles that things will work out, he's not so sure how this will happen.

This Is Me and My Two Families: An Awareness Scrapbook/Journal for Children Living in Stepfamilies by Marla D. Evans (Washington, DC: Magination Press, 1991). If you're going to be living in a stepfamily, this scrapbook/journal is for you. Work on it with your parents, stepparents, grandparents, or stepgrandparents to help you keep track of the important things that are happening in your family's life.

A really important thing to remember, no matter how crazy life may get, is that your mom will always be your mom and your dad will always be your dad. That won't change. Your dad or mom may be with someone new, but there's still a place for you. You belong to your parents, and they belong to you.

All through your life, changes will occur—some big and some small, some negative and some positive. Change can be scary and upsetting. Almost always, though, people get used to the changes in their lives, after they've had some time to adjust or to heal.

Divorce is a change. It's big and scary and new—but it will also bring good things. Your family life may be more peaceful after a divorce. Your parents may be happier. If you eventually get a stepfamily, there will be more people who love you and for you to love. You still have a home and a family. You're still loved, no matter what changes life may bring.

A few final words

Changes are happening, but one thing is the same: *you are special.* Everyone who loves you and everyone you love knows this. No one else in the world is like you. Nothing can ever change the fact that you're special. The divorce can't change that. Sadness can't change that. You *will* feel happy again. It may take time, but it will happen.

You may be feeling as if a hurricane has just blown through your life. Divorces are like those great storms of nature. When a hurricane hits a community, some families' homes may get torn up or blown down. The people in these families are sad and shocked for a while, but they eventually rebuild their homes. The same thing is true about divorces. They're sad and difficult, but as time passes, everyone gets used to the changes and moves forward with their lives.

Talk about the changes and your feelings. Give yourself some time. You *will* get through the divorce and be okay again.

About the authors

Kent Winchester is a trial lawyer who helps women who are sexually harassed and people who are treated unfairly by big corporations. He's the father of two children, Ian and Shauna. He loves to backpack, fly-fish, and read. Kent is the coauthor of *Speaking of Divorce: How to Talk to Your Kids About Divorce and Help Them Cope,* with Roberta Beyer, and is the author of the *Magic Words Handbook for Kids*. He lives in New Mexico and has two border collies.

Roberta Beyer is a lawyer and mediator who helps families through the divorce process. She has always wanted to help kids whose parents are getting divorced, and in 1995, she created a calendar with stickers so kids and parents could keep track of their schedules. Since then, she has developed other products, and along with Kent Winchester, she also wrote *Speaking of Divorce: How to Talk to Your Kids About Divorce and Help Them Cope.* She's the creator of The "Keep Track" Calendar for Kids and The Mom & Dad Pad. Roberta's favorite things to do are fly-fishing, gardening, and cooking. She lives in Albuquerque, New Mexico, with her two border collies, Fly and Jenny, whom she loves to spoil.

Other Materials from Free Spirit Publishing

JUGGLING ACT KIT
Handling Divorce
Without Dropping the Ball:
A Survival Kit for Parents and Kids
This comprehensive kit includes the parents' book, kids' book, Mom & Dad Pad with mailing envelopes, calendar, and stickers. For parents and caregivers of children 12 and under. *$49.95; box is 10" x 13"*

SPEAKING OF DIVORCE
How to Talk to Your Kids and Help Them Cope
by Roberta Beyer and Kent Winchester
Provides information and sample scripts that parents can use to help their children cope with this life-changing experience. For parents and caregivers of children 12 and under. *$10.95; 128 pp.; softcover; illus.; 6" x 6"*

THE MOM & DAD PAD
A Divorce Communication Tool

Divorced parents can use the forms to notify each other about school events, appointments, transportation arrangements, travel plans, and other scheduling issues. For parents and caregivers. *$15.95; 25 forms with carbonless copies; 25 mailing envelopes; 8¹/₂" x 11"*

"KEEP TRACK" CALENDAR FOR KIDS

Kids can fill in this blank calendar with notes and stickers to remind them which parent they'll be with on which days, and helps them keep track of special events, holidays, appointments, homework, and activities. For ages 7–12. *$9.95; 8¹/₂" x 11"*

"KEEP TRACK" STICKERS FOR KIDS

Kids can use these colorful stickers to mark holidays, school activities, and other special dates in calendars. For ages 7–12. *$9.95; set of 400 stickers; each sticker is approximately 1" x 1"*

To place an order or to request a free catalog of SELF–HELP FOR KIDS® and SELF–HELP FOR TEENS® materials, please write, call, email, or visit our Web site:

Free Spirit Publishing Inc.
217 Fifth Avenue North • Suite 200 • Minneapolis, MN 55401-1299
toll-free 800.735.7323 • local 612.338.2068 • fax 612.337.5050
help4kids@freespirit.com • www.freespirit.com

Visit us on the Web!
www.freespirit.com

Stop by anytime to find our Parents' Choice Approved catalog with fast, easy, secure 24-hour online ordering; "Ask Our Authors," where visitors ask questions—and authors give answers—on topics important to children, teens, parents, teachers, and others who care about kids; links to other Web sites we know and recommend; fun stuff for everyone, including quick tips and strategies from our books; and much more! Plus our site is completely searchable so you can find what you need in a hurry. Stop in and let us know what you think!

Just point and click!

new! Get the first look at our books, catch the latest news from Free Spirit, and check out our site's newest features.

contact Do you have a question for us or for one of our authors? Send us an email. Whenever possible, you'll receive a response within 48 hours.

order! Order in confidence! Our secure server uses the most sophisticated online ordering technology available. And ordering online is just one of the ways to purchase our books: you can also order by phone, fax, or regular mail. No matter which method you choose, excellent service is our goal.

1.800.735.7323 • fax 612.337.5050 • help4kids@freespirit.com